Empty the Ocean with a Thimble

Living with Sisu

Empty the Ocean with a Thimble

Living with Sisu

Poems by Elizabeth Kirkpatrick-Vrenios

Word Poetry

Published by Word Poetry
P.O. Box 541106
Cincinnati, OH 45254-1106

ISBN: 9781625493774

Poetry Editor: Kevin Walzer
Business Editor: Lori Jareo

Visit us on the web at www.wordpoetrybooks.com

Table of Contents

Sisu

Finns have a name for it
strength that forges metal
that wields a broom handle
to imprint on a ceiling
it is Sisu

my grandmother Mummo hammered
dints across the tin ceiling
with a broom handle
dints of fire
midnight sun
dark polar nights
full of apron-thin frustration

a streak of madness
formidable
as the aurora borealis
Sisu slips through
the rivers of Karelia
and into my bed
i must tell you i need that shadow
to survive

Notebook, 1906

The belch of the big engine in the ship's belly
is the Kalavala monster in the stories
Papa whispers to me each night. It roars
like the mouth of the river
near the wooden house we left behind.

Coal dust under our nails, in papa's mustache,
between my teeth. Onnie, finally quiet,
sucks on Äiti's breast
and Äiti sings *Laulaa laulaa*.
Cold is everywhere, pressing on us,
even my blue wool *pusero* can't keep me warm.

I miss stones humming silver songs of Kullervo,
the *tuulen* voice that intones the words of Kalevala
and mountains singing the ground that makes my bones
soft with wonder. I miss grass
and the faces of yellow flowers that shiver over my head.
I miss the dirt path that dances up the hill to the sauna,
where Papa's big iron brush
makes the walls smell sweet
like *laipa* that Äiti pulls from the small clay oven.

The horn blows and blows and hurts my ears,
but Papa says that means we are arriving in Amerika.
He holds me up to the round hole in the side of the big boat,
and I see the biggest lady in the world
holding something over her head.

The horn blows, Onnie cries,
Äiti sings. Papa whispers I have to be a good girl
and hold his hand and learn to speak English
when we leave this dark space. I can hardly wait to see
what Amerika will look like.
I hope it has *lumi* like Finland.

Äiti = mother
pusero = sweater
tuulen = wind's
laipa = bread
lumi = snow

Rune #1

Strike the Kantele.
Sing, Mother, Sing,
We are the same, O Mother,
the same inscrutable stars,
we are the same Äiti, O Äiti.

Rose in the Dark

Father performed the morning rites:
waking Mother with a cup of coffee

before rousing me at daybreak
for oatmeal at the green Formica table.

Overhead like a premature sun the naked
bulb hung, flashed its brassy smile,

inviting me into the gold of *soon*
that inched closer each day.

I folded each memory
of Father's morning ritual,

Mother's daily ice storms,
stored them among my lingerie

to trade, in my twenties,
for what seemed like love.

Sauerkraut

At seven I was too tall to stand
in the space my father had dug by hand
under the porch stairs
using tools I could not name.

Wobbly wooden shelves
held jars of thick blackberry jam,
tightly sealed mason jars of peaches,
and pears in syrup
like embryos.

In the center of the dank hole,
squatted a large crock
as grody as the ancient mummy
in last Saturday afternoon's matinee.

Flies buzzed black
over the heavy lid.
thick green mold inside
nasty
as the sweaty crevices
between my toes.

Here was sauerkraut, ripe and juiced,
mud-sour and alien,
the prized platter
at the center of our Finnish Christmas table.

Stare Deep in the Gene Pool

Mother's slotted spoon
   chews circles
inside the saucepan,

its teeth clack on the counter.
   She brews fish heads,
 chops onions.

Her blades cut cankers
   from celery hearts
cruelty and regret.

Beets, the color of blame
    bleed into the restless waters,
scarlet as her daughter's fear.

Twitching fingers
      drum
 impatient tattoos.

Her little girl gorges
     on stars that fall
in showers.

In her chest
   a meadow
startled by magpies.

Five O'-Clock Piano Lesson

I descend into the scent
of old paper and mothballs.
Reluctant and hungry,
Dog-eared *Thompson's 15 Easy Pieces*

clutched tightly to my chest,
perch on a stack of encyclopedias,
nubby covers worn smooth.
Volumes A through E

lift me to the keyboard,
my Buster Browns scuff
the underbelly of the upright,
its dark mahogany-skin

scaled like the rattle snake
father killed in the field behind our house.
Nested on top of the piano,
pungent bananas

overflow a crockery bowl.
Ripe fingers bob time
with my left-hand thump,
reminding me that I'm hungry.

I lose my place, forget the tempo,
doubt the metronome.
Ah! those yellow wags,
chide me for too little practice,

curl their plump banana thumbs,
tempt me: *Eat, eat!*
Late afternoon nudges through lace curtains
slithers across the dark oriental.

I hear the sputter of cars outside the window
returning home to dinner,
still I thump on, metronome, bananas,
metronome, bananas.

My Father Always Hated Cowboy Movies

especially the ones
where the hero wore a hankie
>*A decoration,* he called it,
>*no good for what it does,*
>*a Hollywood frou-frou.*

Those harnesses full of silver
that glittered in the moon light.
>*Too heavy for the horse*
>Pop would say,
>*cuts into the flesh.*

My father rode the range,
before moving pictures
inured us to that hardship.
He squinted into the horizon,

shaded his eyes with his hat
sweat-stained and curled from the sun,
six-shooter in his belt,
a speck of regret in his eye

when he returned to find
his thin-lipped wife
tapping her foot,
waiting.

Practice Makes Perfect

Mother intoned,
thumping with her ruler,

while I struggled at the keys.
I practiced the art of deception,

turning water to ice under a silk scarf,
coaxing my mad dogs beneath the table

to silence their whimper.
In a dream

I carried a dead child on my shoulders,
crept down the darkened hall

to the mirror expecting
a snarling beast with plundered eyes.

But there was nothing
in the shadows.

The hair on the backs of the dogs
began to rise.

But practice doesn't make perfect,
it makes permanent.

While I practiced the art of the silk scarf,
the mad dogs rose, growled and shook their chains.

When I Am Old Enough

I will climb to the top of the tree to hide
and bellow through the applauding leaves
spooning my song like alphabet soup
into the open mouths of upturned faces.
I will lie in fields of mustard and lupine
and they will grow catawampus over my head
and hide me in their open hands.
And when the nip of the willow switch stings,
I will not cry. I will not cry.

I will peer out at clouds until the dark grows tall,
birds stop singing
and stars pull me up past their pinpoints
to spaces beyond spaces
and I am in the deep alone.
And I will never, ever
have to go home
ever again.

Rune #2

O Mother, O Äiti we are lightning,
slicing the sky. O Mother, O Äiti,
we are the iron earth that breaks
the ploughshare,
the same, you and I.

Morning Glories

I awake and the world has changed:
muddy water wrinkles everywhere,
our home is a houseboat,
the driveway a lake,

the field of morning glories gone.
Trees lift their skirts
like young girls tiptoeing
through mud.

When the river rises to their armpits,
my brothers haul out their homemade kayak
and whoop and paddle to the barn
to rescue the cow.

I love the muddy new landscape:
fold tiny paper boats,
watch them ripple to the barn
where water lifts straw from its sleep.

All the while the flood
laps at the front steps,
eating its way to the door.

Our Home Before the Split

My father perches
on the peak of the house.
Smoke curls from his pipe

mixes with the pungent aroma
of new lumber, sawdust,
entwining sweet burn with pine musk.

In three unstoppable hammer swings
he coaxes the nail's black pinpoint
easily into the wood's flesh.

The buzz of the circular saw
rings through the rafters,
splitting the bones of the house open.

It cuts into the years,
pulls apart decades
now exposed to the clear November light.

Two rough halves,
of mother and father
share the grain's internal darkness.

The wood resists,
hesitates a moment, until at last
it transforms into new geometry.

Saturday Matinee at the Avon Theater, 1951

What have I done, that for the first time
I hear the sweet thunder of your heart?
Robert Taylor to Deborah Kerr in *Quo Vadis*

We fifth graders tolerated the newsreels,
imitated the pretentious voice intoning
    Time   Marches   On
waiting to give the cartoons our roar of approval
as we chanted in unison at the top of our voices:
    abbada abbada abbada That's all Folks!
One story ran into another.
Large in our own universe,
we could not imagine a world beyond
Big Hunks and Walnettos, The Bowery Boys and Jungle Jim.

I learned about yearning and love
on those shadowed afternoons,
when affection mushroomed
for cowboys on white horses,
gladiators slaying lions,
and Tarzan swinging from the trees.

When the last reel flapped itself up,
we emerged into the bright blink.
None of us could know how life
would scatter us like milkweed
seeds in the breeze,
we only knew sunlight,
and our long shadows home.

One-Room Schoolhouse

My task: to take the black felt erasers
outside and clap them together,
obliterating the little cursive *O*'s
and curly cues of *L*'s and *Y*'s
in chalk clouds,
leaving my braids
and the front of my jumper white
with math
and history.

Carved initials covered my desk,
MK loves DS, embedded so deep
in the middle of a heart it seemed
love's survival was certain.
I longed to mark my own
with Robbie Petrocelli's.

Remember me in the cobwebs,
four-year-old believer
in fairy tales. Remember
me in the school-bell
ringing its joy from the pull of a rope,
the tall mustard and rust
abandon of the swing set.

Who Put Rocks in the Gas Tank?

She wants you to lie, Little Miss Five Alive,
admit to a deed that was never you.
It begins with a swarm of black flies & a shiver
of a girl,
locked in a car by her mother,
slivered darkness
inside - - the white room
dark & in the dark room
curtains whisper, they buzz,
lies of black
flies folded inside.

Crawl *Little Crumb that Falls*
crawl on the floor,
floor hard as wishes, crawl
to kettle of lye, to taste of soap–
inside-soap, cement tub, wringer
slick with red– -crawl,
Little Hairline Crack,

break the bottle black
as flies, break
black lies skin blue-
edged & inside, blackened eye,
eye of wolf, beaten
& locked inside the car. Grab
Little Miss Never Heard, grab the goat-
haired wig & red eye of mother.
Even a wolf can smell the blood of a lie.

Little Pile of Rags, do you know who you are?
Too many times you tried to pass
as a freckle of tar,
but Mother tries to strip a lie from you
& beat it into blood-black, beat
you into lies. Shake,
Little Speck of Star.
Shake the buzz from the curtains,
let fables fly out the window, free
them like trapped flies, *Little Teaspoon of Honey.*
Bury your truth *Little Tatter of Song,*
keep the startle quiet, quiet
inside the locked car.
Inside the padlocked garage

After a Particularly Dark Day

I sit before the piano's
>> gap-toothed grin
>>>> my fingers hesitate

on this scaled
>> creature who wears
>>>> a plumed Papageno hat

we begin the rollick
>> I command
>>>> the white Mozart flag

 toss the Papageno hat
>> aloft
>>>> feathers pirouette

tickling
>> in a language
>>>> that is irresistible

I brandish my wooden Mozart sword
>> parade over the keyboard
>>>> in yellow Mozart boots

sing in squishes
>> and splurts
>>>> jump

in the middle
>> of each musical
>>>> puddle

joy wriggles
      its Mozart fingers
           hangs

catty-cornered
      from the left ear
           of the crescent moon

Little Miss Third Birthday

The shoes were not just any shoes, but
licorice-shiny patent leather,
Remember, her mother warned, *they are special,*
not ever for outside.

When she put them on, she was transformed,
wreathed in light, dancing from star to star,
wings on the buckles, kisses soft on her feet.

Burn the shoes sang: *Burn Little-Blonde-Briar,*
 Burn Little-Bonfire,
 lift your embers to your desire.

Bright as a moonstone she napped,
not brown-scuffed, laced-up,
but fairy borne.

Winged voices sang: *You will be what you will be,*
 but remember, little mouse,
 never wear us outside the house.

*

The day dawned, birthday-bright,
full of promise, sunlight,
and alone with Father
her first movie,
Bambi.

 Wear us, the shoes crooned.
 Wear us. This is a special ballyhoo.
 Let us sing and dance for you.

She listened,
carefully placed her toes
inside the soft leather,
scampered through the forest,
laughed with Thumper and Flower,
gamboled with Bambi

but sobbed against father's shoulder
when Bambi's mother
perished in the fire.

Shiny shoes laughed, *Outrun the fire*
    Little Miss-Burning-Fawn
    unbury the mother,
    unbreak the sky.

*

Behind the swirled thickets
mother's eyes flared,
she met the girl at the door
with wooden spoon in her fist.

The depths of the forest floor pursued the girl,
rose up to meet her.
She tried to fly

but there was only the cracked song of right and left:
    You wore us outside,
    Little Fragile-Water,
    we can't give you wings.
    Little Silent-Spring.

First Schwinn

Our shadows behind,
the sun gold in our faces,
your hand on the blue fender,
running beside me.

Hold me up!
Holy Moly!
I'm on my own!

We reel down the street,
your blue gaze vigilant
from beneath a battered fedora.

Freedom vibrates through the pedals,
cuts into my Keds,
turns my Dutch braids into wings.

The road unravels,
I am unsteady, waver,
surprised by my own unfolding.

Your hand suddenly gone,
yet the distant ribbon of your voice
holds me steady
as I wobble down the pavement
drawing unsteady lines with fat tires.

Sixty years later
you are still there, Father,
shading your eyes with your soft-brimmed hat,
your voice steady, persistent,
Fly, Sugarpuss, fly!

I Hold My Childhood Picture

Little Blue- Checked Girl,
fling your doll
against early spring azaleas
where bees gather soft packages of dawn.

You race toward me,
Little Wiggly Tow Head,
Little Greenly Two,
Little Honey Toes.

I watch over you
Little Rock Who Soars,
you will struggle to empty
the ocean with a thimble.

Little Twig Who Snaps Under Sorrow's Shank,
I know you will cut out your tongue
and feed it to crows, I know you will bury
your heart in the ground.

Little Doll Who Breaks.
I want to tell you: wrap your arms
around your sorrows,
ride joy until it shatters like glass.

Breathe your own river,
and swim, swim!
Little Trout Who Laughs,
Little Carousel,
Little Singing Bell.

Vanishing Acts

1.

when I disappeared
the neighborhood did not gather
to look for me
they did not drag the river
they did not dig under the lush camellia
they did not   look   in the oven
where I left a clue
          of salt and bone ash

I wasn't   in the bird cage
lying next   to   my yellow canary
nor was   I entombed
with the summer's jarred
peaches on shelves in the garage
I   wasn't   under   the sink
in the little Dutch girl's
blue dress   wasn't
in the Morton maid's
trail of salt

2.

Where am I now, Mother?
Do I live in the   dint
between your   forefinger
and   thumb?

Like a ruined town
I've burned my name off your map
nailed my carcass
to your tree   mother
where the wind rings
through me

Rune #3

I wear you like a cheerless jacket,
distant and blue, Oh Äiti,
you row through the slots
in my bones.

I See You Mother

at the end of the hall   watching me
hidden   in the shadows
rocking silently   watching
as grandfather once watched
hidden   in shadows
silently   smoking   watching his daughters
hoping to see   a hand up a dress
a quick pee in the corner
his hand on his crotch

Mother sits now
silent   cold   a gunmetal sky chair
facing my door
without my knowing
watches me
plots   smiles
when my boyfriend enters
my bedroom

as you did when I was small
your ear pressed to my door
hoping to hear   a wicked
part of me   revealed
you wanted the heat
and slick of me

I have read of wicked Queens
and cruel stepmothers
        but learned
in real life they are a gamble
Only if you lose life's lottery
do you get one
        one who will hum and think
and plot and smile
and rock.

I Never Saw My Father Cry

except once.
My words lashed against his flesh,
a sharp-tipped whip.

In a teenaged tantrum of self-righteous pique,
I tried to break him down
as he dropped his head in his hands.

How many times have I thought to ask forgiveness?

That pain still
shadows me, I see him bent at the table,
tears on his cheeks, silent.

Consider Your Malice a Minor Disaster,

a stitch dropped, a tied naught, a hole singular,
what did it matter what might not come after?

You're a factor of nothing, a sum of no matter
a flat spot's blind crack behind tuneless guitars.
I considered your rancor a minor disaster.

But love's cloaks, torn open, discarded in tatters,
bumblebee's sting and wasp's repertoire
taught me it mattered what clatter came after.

The choke and the blow are your fury's cruel masters,
a dusky eclipse, a gnarled icy gnarr,
your malice, I learned, a certain disaster.

Your knot of self-loathing destroyed you much faster
than memory's last gasp or my fuddled memoir,
for it no longer matters what might not come after.

You've shrunk down much smaller, you're no longer vaster.
The heat of your ego can no longer scar.
I consider your sickness a feeble disaster
and yes! Oh yes, Mother, a lifetime comes after.

Your Face in the Mirror

She was a stranger,
now only body, vein and bone.
I had become an outlander,
come to kneel

in the unbuckled light, split
with the grief of my beginning.
I was dusty and howling,
not from the sadness of her departure,

but for the want of her love.
How can I describe
love's grim silk,
deep enough to drown in.

Like the candle burning on the kitchen table,
Mother, I still think I can extinguish you.
See? Just a pinch
you are gone.

All I Wanted

In mother's room
my brothers and I stand beside
her bed, trying to feel anything
for this dead woman we barely recognize.

I had rushed from the plane
responding to a hurried call
of *Come quickly, if you want to see her.*
No one spoke above a whisper,
the silence thick about our ears
as each of us held back
what we were thinking.

At that moment I was four,
dressed in mother's oversized lime-green dress,
running through the back yard,
to feel the mud through my toes
and kneel at the overturned wooden box
to examine the mud pies
I had left baking in the sun.

My brothers and I needed to leave,
needed to breathe, walk, anything,
perhaps go to dinner
and a movie. We all felt guilty
for leaving her in her bed,
The only relief was
a comedy at the Roxy.
Robyn Williams and a rare hamburger
was exactly what we needed
the day mother died.

Flooded

I stand   at the top of the porch
watch the   Manzanita trunks
sweep   by my window
        no longer able to resist
the push of the   Russian River

Bared roots like   black fingers
point   to the sky
empty chairs   chrome tables   tumble
planks   drift
against the walls of that damp house

where mold shadows   mirrors
        curtains   shudder
where life smells   of stones   and vinegar
Under my feet   a persistent thunder
Mother   I try to take it in   wanting to record
in a poem about you   I would write someday
                I was that ruthless

ACKNOWLEDGMENTS

My thanks to the editors of the following magazines in which some of these poems previously appeared, sometimes in a different format.

Duck Lake Books: Stare into the Gene Pool
Poetry Barn: One Room School House
Comstock Review: This is the Story as I Tell it (Who Put Rocks in the Gas tank?)
Minnie's Diary Naming Mother Bi-Polar (Little Miss Third -Birthday) (nominated Pushcart Prize)
Oyster River Review: Practice Makes Perfect
Front Porch Review: The Truth About Childhood (Rose in the Dark)
Passager Journal Contest runner up: I Hold My Childhood Picture
Stories of Music: Piano at Five
Red Fez: Father Teaching Me (First Schwinn)
Silkworm: Childhood was Not What She Thought (Rose in the Dark)
Silver Birch Press: When I Am Old Enough
Fish Food : Sauerkraut
Existere Journal of Arts and Literature: Morning Glories

Elizabeth Kirkpatrick-Vrenios is professor emerita from American University in Washington DC, having chaired the vocal and music departments. Vrenios' solo recitals throughout the US, South America, Scandinavia, Japan and Europe have been acclaimed. Featured in Tupelo Press's 30/30 challenge, she has been published in such journals as *Great Weather for Media, Cumberland River Review, The Feminine Collective, The Kentucky Review, Edison Literary review, Passager, NILVX, Unsplendid, The Ekphrastic Review* and featured in such anthologies as *The Poeming Pigeon, Love Notes from Humanity, Stories of Music* and *The American Journal of Poetry*, and was nominated for a Pushcart Prize. Her chapbook *Special Delivery*, prize winner with Yellow Chair Press, was published in 2016. As the artistic director of the Redwoods Opera in Mendocino, California, she has influenced and trained vocal students across the country. She lives and writes next to the sea in Mendocino, California.

Made in the USA
Monee, IL
30 April 2021